CW01336986

Words Without Song

VIGNETTES OF REFLECTIVE DISSENT AND CHILDHOOD RECOLLECTIONS

Martin Knox

authorHOUSE

AuthorHouse™ UK
1663 Liberty Drive
Bloomington, IN 47403 USA
www.authorhouse.co.uk
Phone: UK TFN: 0800 0148641 (Toll Free inside the UK)
   UK Local: 02036 956322 (+44 20 3695 6322 from outside the UK)

© 2020 Martin Knox. All rights reserved.

No part of this book may be reproduced, stored in a retrieval system, or transmitted by any means without the written permission of the author.

Published by AuthorHouse 30/06/2020

ISBN: 978-1-7283-5445-3 (sc)
ISBN: 978-1-7283-5444-6 (e)

Print information available on the last page.

Any people depicted in stock imagery provided by Getty Images are models, and such images are being used for illustrative purposes only.
Certain stock imagery © Getty Images.

This book is printed on acid-free paper.

Because of the dynamic nature of the Internet, any web addresses or links contained in this book may have changed since publication and may no longer be valid. The views expressed in this work are solely those of the author and do not necessarily reflect the views of the publisher, and the publisher hereby disclaims any responsibility for them.

Dedication

For My Family

Contents

Preface	xi
Introduction	xiii
Finding a Voice:	1
Feeding the Crows:	3
Cairo 2007	4
The Greasy Till	5
The Beginning of the Summer of 2012:	7
Impending Blindness:	9
Brother Romanus	10
The Markets	11
Indoctrination at the Moral Sciences Club, Cambridge 1946:	12
Science Lesson 1	13
Science Lesson 2:	15
Love	16
The Ostler	17
The Agnostic	18
The Penal Code, Sharia Law Interpreted:	19
The Secularist	21
Feeding the Virus	22
The Camino	23
Indoctrination 2:	24
Grandma's Treats	26
Serving Mass	27
The Coffin Ship,	28
Ag Críost an Síol	29
DIP 312:	30
Granny Smyth	31
A Memory	33

A Hibernian Holocaust,	34
Sunday Break:	35
Anzac Day,	36
Flamingos Feeding,	37
Going to the Pump,	38
On Reading Kavanagh's Poems	39
The Bomb,	40
The Death of Cleopatra	41
A Safe Pair of Hands	42
The Willy Week,	43
Life and Death:	44
The Endgame	45
Drones:	46
Fear	48
Out West:	50
Bells:	51
The Lime Kiln	53
Lucy	55
Ineluctable Conclusions:	56
Never Count the Dead	59
The Faith Healer	61
Spanish Neanderthals	62
Chilly Winds	63
Mescaline Haze	64
Sharing Wealth	65
The Deniers	66
Failures	69
The Alien One:	70
Pandering to Illusions	71
Winter	72
Getting Over It	73
Night Flight	75
Go Figure:	77

The Christmas Cake	79
The Proclamation Remembered	80
The National Debt Revisited:	82
Pain	84
Early Spring Flowers:	85
The End of Music	87
On a Trip to Abu Dhabi	88
DJ: Hurling Wizard	90
Gödel's Theorem	91
The E Major Chord	92
The Man with the Beard in Café 9:	93
Moments of Reprieve:	95
Labels	96
Hobbes, Hugo, and Hume	97
The Ohakune Train	98
Early Autumn Bush Sounds:	99
A Hidden Legacy	100
Forgotten:	102
On a Train to Bournemouth	103
A Royal Entitlement	104
Powerlessness	106
Here Comes the Sun	107
Wasted on Margaritas in Dublin, Early Sixties	108
Fulfilment of a Dream:	111
Science, Religion and Urban Myths	112
Alan Kurdi:	113
Family Matters	115
Travails	116
The Entropy Class	117
Removing the Filters	118
A Sunday Morning Dawdle:	119
Terezin, Destination:	121

Late Breakfast	122
Union Station, Kansas City,	123
The Woman on the 229 Bus,	125
God, Guns, and Paranoia	126
Making Hay:	127
Rock Salt	129
Chavs:	130
It's Not Dark Yet	131
Seeking Patterns	132
An Old Man:	133
An Army Vet Runs for Congress	135
An Evening of Ale and Rashers	136
The Corpulent Canon	138
Slings and Guns	139
Kelly's Crag:	140
Settled Bread and Craven A	141
The Triumph of Nothingness	143
Churros in a Chiringuito	144
Anzac Memory, April 1915	146
Phosphorus Bombs on the Gaza Strip	147
Hamilton Gardens, 18 February 2019	148
Holding Back the Tide	149
The Living Wind	150
Alone and Old	151
A Snifter Break	152
A Childhood Dream:	153
Winter Fuel	156
A Foolish Enterprise	157
Swan Lake Conversations:	158
When I Was Ten	160
Looking at a Mansion	161
Filtering Out the Lies:	162
About the Author	165

Preface

This book has had a gestation period of approximately ten years. The inspiration for the book derives, to a considerable degree, from personal experiences as well as from the work of other writers such as Noam Chomsky, Primo Levi, Bertrand Russell, Bob Dylan, Paddy Kavanagh, and Michael Hartnett, together with encounters of various kinds, but more especially from life's experiences.

The quality of governance worldwide is variable. I'm trying to be as kind as I possibly can be here. My poems echo the environment in which we live by drawing attention to a multitude of unnecessary pain arising in the main from how we govern ourselves and relying heavily on our belief systems. It is, I believe, one of our obligations as writers to expose this pain and its causes in the belief that we can ease that generated by those who pursue wealth generation at the expense of humanity and the earth's resources. In most economies, it is wealth that matters, not people. It's a pity that we don't work on social cohesion with the same energy and resolve.

As I write, we are in the midst of a global pandemic, a wake-up call to us all to prepare for and pre-empt global catastrophes. Its potential devastation was flagged by many, including Barack Obama and Bill Gates. Yet we prefer to consume scarce resources on building armaments promoting empty fashion instead of preparing for well-flagged, realistic catastrophes heading our way. Climate change science is solid. If there's ground for scepticism, well then, let's have it. Deniers are malevolent.

In my poetry I try to highlight the issues which I see as potentially catastrophic for humanity and Mother Earth. As I write, we are governed by those perhaps not with full-blown narcissism but with tendencies towards the affliction. Where leaders are narcissists, people suffer. Long-term planning is neglected for short-term 'gains'. The narcissistic leader, namely one who is entirely caught up in himself, is incapable of empathy, incapable of imagining the plight of others, and incapable of fixing real societal problems. The single-minded obsession of many rulers with power and wealth are often nurtured by the wealthy, who through bribery and corruption have a disproportionate influence on important decision-making, such as those decisions around oil, coal, oxygen (rarely mentioned), and other limited natural resources. The wealthy arrogate to themselves earth's assets unhindered, all the while dumping their wastes in waterways, groundwater, the atmosphere, and soil. If we continue along this path, we will see unrelenting species elimination, including humankind. That is an unquestionable outcome, and we owe it to potential future generations to stop the rape of the planet forthwith.

Some of the poems derive from childhood memories. With some exceptions (Granny Smyth who died in 1955), all other characters imagined by the reader in these poetic snapshots are just that, characters imagined by the reader and will not in any way correspond with those dreamt up by the writer. Imagined characters are, of course, just that: imagined.

Introduction

In this book of one hundred-plus poems, I try to raise awareness of the many enormous injustices in the world through accessible and naïve writing, without, at the same time, fully interpreting the poems for the reader. Tyrannical governance ought to have no place in our world, and raising consciousness about such tyrannies is, in my view, the concern of the writer. Needless to say, therefore, my poetry is not pro-establishment; that would be a betrayal and hypocritical. It is indeed devastating to discover that social engineering has succeeded to such an extent that a small elite control the planet and its resources. The forces running counter to acquired and inherited privilege are so weak and pathetic as to be imperceptible. We are sold the hopelessly vain promise that you can be a millionaire if, like the proponent, you are smart; that is, you don't pay your suppliers and so put them out of business, or similarly, by not paying taxes and or by exploiting of employees. We must nail that lie. Supporting and marketing goods which add little value to life and liberty while promoting consumerism through empty advertisements is destructive and should be limited through carbon-footprint taxing or sustainable carbon-footprint allowances for every citizen on the planet.

The most important function of state is likely to be education, and most states fail miserably to deliver a service which upholds the principles of liberty that promote participative governance, freedom of thought, and analytical thinking. Most if not all educational endeavours are driven by the potential to acquire wealth and status as well as the acquisition of questionable values, instead of the value of authentic living, rationality, independent thinking, and creativity.

So many human pursuits are almost entirely empty. Such pursuits have very little to offer and are too often allowed to masquerade as genuine scientific endeavour; pseudo-science is rampant of course. Many human pursuits—such as theology, psychology, psychiatry, economics, astrology, alternative medicine, and politics—masquerade as rigorous scientific endeavours, but they are: the methodology of the scientific method is largely ignored altogether or is only partially deployed. One of the major challenges in the application of the scientific method, is the use of the control experiment: the background must be understood, incorporated and controlled. Opinion and party allegiance-jabber are not science. Much of what we hear and experience in social encounters, over the airwaves, in the print media, and from the pulpit is not informed through the furnace of rational analysis or freedom of thought and has the potential to harm the unsuspecting mind. Evidence-based judgements are, in reality, all that matter; the rest is noise. If there is no evidence for the entity presented, then it does not exist. Propaganda is usually delivered by those who have an axe to grind and who have not been through the mill of well-honed interrogation of assumptions and the demanding discipline of rigorously informed scepticism.

Pseudo-science and attendant soul-destroying noise are rampant, thereby dragging authentic science into the gutter. The latter is robust but can falter, of course, when soberingly, counterexamples to one's treasured hypotheses are found. There is no place for dogma in its pursuit. For example, it is worth reflecting on the achievements of Robert Boyle. Emanating from his law—Boyle's law—is the concept of the ideal gas.

This law postulates that the pressure of a gas is inversely proportional to its volume, assuming a fixed quantity of gas at a fixed temperature. That is to say, when you double the pressure, the volume of the gas halves. He discovered this relationship about 350 years ago. Real gases (oxygen, sulphur dioxide, and so on) do not obey this law under ambient conditions and deviate from the ideal pressure-volume relationship, especially as the pressure increases. That's science! Does the ideal gas have the same status as, say, a guardian angel? Interesting question and worth mulling over.

The reading of poetry is sobering, rewarding, and enjoyable. Not everyone will agree with the views expressed herein, but so what? Disagreements are part of the fun of life, and omniscience is very thin on the ground. But no one has the right to push dogma on anyone else, either at the point of a gun or by using other chilling threats. Forcing dogma through the use of fear is the ultimate manifestation of tyranny.

September 2020

Finding a Voice:

A Wakeful Dream

I met a wayward victim in a crowded city street
Just as the sun was peeping through
The grey-upholstered dawn.
Nothing is black or white, but mostly grey.
The sufferer was reflecting deeply
While perusing the breaking day.

I didn't know what to say;
I didn't know where to look
As the victim shouted sobriquets
While reading from a sacred book.

Nigra sum sed Formosa*
—King Solomon's lustful urge—
Finds words in song,
An uncontrollable surge
Of DNA-enhanced adrenaline.

The wisest man who had ever lived
Controlled seven hundred wives,
Three hundred native concubines.
Though strangely, none felt vicariously deceived.

Who was this Solomon?
How dare he take advantage of nefarious power
And casually deflower
So many.
It was the effects of separation.

Or was it a way of reflecting on a stodgy world,
And life had now become unfurled?

Our eyes met.
Had we met somewhere else before?
I began to fret ... and sweat.
Do we have a history?
Or are we looking for something more,
Something I cannot give?

*I am black but beautiful

Feeding the Crows:

A Funeral Trip to Cork

The cawing crows carelessly feed on errant cracked corn,
Scattered serendipitously along that busy cavernous road;
Exposed cores are splintered and milled
By traffic wheels
West of Cork city.
As we travelled to encounter the solemn man with
The bowler hat and Crombie coat,
On another day out for the Grim Reaper.

Cairo 2007

At last we can
Take time out now
To reflect
On the enormity of man's achievements!
The pyramids
Testify,
Like the magnificent Blue Mosque, to such.
Built by mortals standing proud;
Or were there gods, unknown to us as we slept,
Raising seven-tonne blocks stealthily
To the clouds?

The Greasy Till

> Steal a little and they throw you in jail,
> steal a lot and they make you king
>
> —Bob Dylan

It is all true, yes—all true.
Much has been lost,
Jarring our beliefs.
Land fought and died for
Lifted seamlessly by thieves
Who walk free, let off
With bonuses.

We must be happy
To be back in the markets
To deal with the flinty highway men—
Those highly respected
(We're so easily duped)—
And a dead republic;
Our children scattered.
Repeated betrayals
Of our ancient heritage
By those elected.

I know of a case—
Her children without food—
Condemned to jail
For lifting rashers

From a respected chain
Of greasy-till merchants.

And what's a sweetheart like you
Doing in a dump like this?

The Beginning of the Summer of 2012:
The Rio Sarela, Galicia, Spain

While breathing the early summered, musky air
And imbibing the aromatic dampness of the scrub,
We wandered reflectively past ferns and nettles,
Alders, oaks, and the familiar birch
To the next Roman bridge or *taberna* or church
Along the translucent Rio Sarela.

Our taberna is cool on a June day.
The beer too.
Midday rest for workers,
Smoking outside now
As they imbibe white and red
From aged *tazas*.

The tannery is long defunct.
We speculate about the rates of pay,
The sorrowful, servile working scene,
And the length of a numbing day.

The humidity, heat, and illness,
The acts of contrition
They regularly say
As they remove animal hair
By the river's edge
While
Holding crushing, aching hunger dolefully at bay.

Minnows dart towards a wayward grub;
The water's crystal clear
Where pilgrims rested—
Travel-weary, sore-footed,
Hungry, ill,
No cure or exit from the vile morass.
Eyes blinded to substantive questions
By a highly illuminated and cerebrally bedazzling looking glass.
Penance,
Plenary indulgences,
High mortality, or deep, deep pain.
Heavy burdens,
Heaven weeps;
The sky is charged with fire and rain.
We're in a bubble
Again today.

Impending Blindness:
Christy, the Birthday Boy

Our winter light is fading fast;
The grey, sad eyes are dimmed.
A foggy veil is drawn
Across scarcely discernible pupils—
Time-worn, trimmed.
The hand is moving in a clumsy way,
Feeling for support.
At eighty-four, he can't afford to fall,
And certainly not today.

Brother Romanus

Profoundly deaf
With thundering voice,
Holy habit's spotted with traces of stale egg
And choice stuff
Mixed with snuff.
Up at five
To suspend disbelief,
To pray, to mediate, to meditate,
To extend a meaningful day,
To advance a religious ideal,
To change the world,
To highlight its woes
For God
With unquestioning zeal.
Indifferent to cruel, nefarious practices.

Caritas Christi urget nos*
*The love of Christ urges us. St Paul, 2 Corinthians 5:14

The Markets

Ah, yes,
The markets are the gods
We must obey
Or feel the pangs of doleful deprivation every day.

The banker buys dependable bonds,
But for the privileged few.
The world is in debt,
But in debt to who?
The body politic
Hums the tune
Of the markets that decide
How best to fool when all is lost.
The citizens whom the bankers chide
For profligacy with their spoils.
And oh, the human cost!

And what do we now do
To avoid another bloodless foreign coup?

Indoctrination at the Moral Sciences Club, Cambridge 1946:

Are There Philosophical Problems?

Wittgenstein's brandished poker,
Popper's empirical concerns,
Original thinkers of substance,
Flinty protagonists,
Colossal egos,
Austrian giants,
Name and reference,
Language puzzles,
And not hemmed in,
Thank God.

The meeting of minds waiting for a subtle fix
At the Moral Sciences Club, Cambridge, England,
In 1946.

Just look through the window
To solve the puzzle
If there is one!

https://www.youtube.com/watch?v=vBmt2sCdd5E.

Science Lesson 1

Are muons the invention of the frenzied?
Do leptons offer any food for thought?
Are such existential affirmations the requisites of fools?
Or are they torrent strong?
Is it always black or white
Until something goes profoundly wrong?

Are these inventions just illusions?
Like phlogiston, one of three kinds of Becher earth,
A non-contradictory set of observations
Feeding twentieth-century scornful mirth.

Theses shoehorned by scientific brains
To be self-referring with unintended circularity,
Uncontrolled and dangerous thoughts
Lacking in compelling uniformity.

'Bah humbug,' cries my friend.
'Science is solid; science is deep.
Some of the greatest stories ever penned
Record advances that we keep

Wrapped up inside,
Against the tide of scepticism
And the mindless, tedium of deniers
With whom we must, in time, collide.'

'The Bohr atom is real,' he says.
'What about our convoluted DNA—
The perfect cubic saline structure—
The reality of curds and whey?'

And again, 'Don't forget
The streptomycin wonder drug
That halted the TB curse
And the speed of light,
The infra-red,
Darwinism, and
Sir Paul Nurse.'

Science Lesson 2:

Terra Pinguis—Phlogiston

Terra Pinguis was Becher's thought,
Alarmed at losing grip
On those holding on
To 'firmer' ground (afraid he'd slip).
He exercised his mind.
A new element to explain
The realm of fire and maybe even rain.
And save the theory
For fear of losing face
Or worse, to vanish without a trace.

Those were dangerous times;
Theology, alchemy's sister, reigned.
Apologists, theologically trained,
Ruled the roost.
It was dangerous to dissent;
Creative energy fretfully misspent.

Love

It's disconcerting and perplexing
To deliberate on love amongst us carefree males.
Love defies description,
But Corinthians 1 lifts a lid.
Love is boundless;
The vessel always overflows.
While I shift from foot to foot,
Eyes cast down uncomfortably, face hid,
Words absurdly fail
To encompass what can be only shown,
Not said, no words.
Words destroy
The emotions.
The vessel always overflows.
It can't be filled.
Language is more than words.
It's all we've got.
Nothing else.
No, nothing,
Nothing,
Nothing!
Well maybe Wittgenstinian pictures.

The Ostler

A cruel unthinking brute,
A mean, low thug
With hair of mouldy hay
Betrayed the lovers.
Jealous,
Dog in the manger,
Sad, cruel,
Unfeeling.
A spoiler of Olympic gold;
An uninvited runner on the track
Of love
Of the landlord's daughter,
Jess.

The Agnostic

There's nothing to believe.
Aye, nothing.
Except there is nothing to believe.
No necessary truths,
None theologic,
No observation, no closed hypotheses.
The senses fool us; we're adrift,
Groping in a darkened room
Or cave with no way out.
And then we sleep;
We dream, tossed on a sea of confusion
And awaken from the nightmare to vacuity and emptiness.

The 'learned' indoctrinate the young
With myths they wish were true
To support a reckless, wayward tongue
With talismanic and emblematic colour codes,
Alternative facts and pseudoscience imbued
With a racist flag—
Red, white, and ensign blue.

The Penal Code, Sharia Law Interpreted:

Article 104,

The Death of Zahra, 2012

In 2012,
In free Iran, the stoning persists
Under an official and hideous tyrannical plan.
Laid out in its code
Of penal bans
Attaching arbitrarily to false dilemmas.

The size of stone
Deployed in the rite
Is not too large
Or small
(To ease her plight)
For fear death might come too soon,
Or despairingly, not at all.

In advance of sacred stoning,
Rubrics planned,
The convict is buried, standing
Fretfully
Deep in a rulebook-specified, constricting sand.
Depth defined up to her neck.
She can't turn 'round or sit.
Can't plead with her killers, no!

The law requires the use of stones
Of measured size.
Thus chillingly
Gruesome, ghastly death
Must come crushingly slow.

The Secularist

Profoundly deaf
With thundering voice
And traces of egg
On the grey lapel mixed with ash.
He's up at six
To reflect and extend the day,
To resume disbelief,
To expand the mind,
Undermine the irrational,
And maybe even change the world
For humankind.

Feeding the Virus

She made a greater concession today
Because she could.
There was no authorisation,
No accountability,
No retribution.
Vicarious plans were realised;
Needs were met.
It was payback time.

The virus lives on,
Proliferates,
Nourished in our tax-exempt greasy till.

The Camino

Try to imagine believers,
Folks of faith,
On rugged roads,
In searing heat,
On steep inclines,
Halting at every altar
And at isolated, man-made, wayside shrines
To atone for sins
Of no consequence.
Confessions regularly made
And a stipend paid
To enrich a furtive power.
Sore, blistered feet,
Faces burnt,
Aching limbs,
Forsaken but granted absolution
To support a tyranny
That holds the mind in thrall
To the gods of fear and retribution.

Indoctrination 2:

Feeding the Virus

What is it now
That makes us acquiesce
In accepting that which we shouldn't
For fear of retribution if we don't do
What the divines say we should?
It is mandated
There must be no danger
To the established order.
No threat from dissenting voices
As the herd combines
To trample the anxious infidel underfoot.
That heretic deserves to die!
Ah, yes,
To make the world a safer place
For those who feel they must conform to
The perceived, ever-expanding demands of
Holy books.
Invented by man,
Emerging from the womb
Of evolution
Terrorised
And recklessly used by rulers
To harness the resource
That is man's labour
To build the pyramids,

The magnificent Baroque churches,
The Blue Mosque,
The splendid palaces,
To keep the capricious tyrant
In control.

Grandma's Treats

(Inspired by Killone Lough)

Sweet cake
With cream
And chunky, warm apple underneath;
You know what I mean.
For Grandma on cold days,
A treat;
She is obstinately set in her ways.

The fog is down now,
Suspended lightly
Over grey water,
Underneath leaden skies.
I saw her on her way to town
To shop
For sherry.

Serving Mass

Seven o'clock,
An early start for a lad
With unquestioned fealty tied
To the mechanical rubrics
And Vatican standards
Universally applied.
Answers off pat, with words that are gentle, docile, tame
In ecclesiastical Latin,
Ad Deum qui laetificat
Juven tutum meum.

*To God who gives joy to my youth.

The Coffin Ship,

May 1847

On a becalmed and sunny summer's day,
She ploughed across
The grey Atlantic,
Leaving Dublin in early May,
Forty-seven,
Heading north, then west
Throughout the summer.
Away from the landlord and the crushing hunger,
The iniquitous alien tithes,
The windswept scraws,
The penal laws
To the promised land,
Replete with the means of production.
Steerage brims with fevered,
Starving, forlorn victims
Set for better times.
There's no water to quench the thirst,
Nor chlorine to dull the stench
Of human misery and decay.
The Brexit of another day.

Hope fades.
Death comes knocking daily,
Sweet, sweet, restful death at terrible cost.
Another white man's burden,
Another Hibernian holocaust.

Ag Críost an Síol

(A childhood memory)

That perfect James Grieve,
Formed from rich, light-brown Clara soil
Without blemish,
Without spoil,
Surviving the winter frosts,
The scab,
The canker,
And the pesky crow;
The busy, harried blackbird knows.

We are treated to a vision of russet and green,
A perfect taste, a perfect shape, and rightful name,
With glossy, polished, mottled skin.
And then
In time, the honey fungus came.

DIP 312:

Going to a Dog Track Sometime in 1958—Sic Transit Gloria Mundi

Clifden Rocket,
Dusty Trail,
Gun-metal grey,
Straw laid out sparsely in the back
For animal comfort
And to stop the rattles.
An unfailing theme
Along rough roads to Enniscorthy
Sustained by a long-held, Derby dream.
Cat's eyes
And poteen,*
Tired muscles relaxed,
Guaranteed to work.

Twenty-nine sixty,
Heavy going,
Best time of the night,
Best time of his life.
Sic Transit Gloria Mundi

*Great rub for a dog.

Granny Smyth

(Nee Kavanagh, born Dublin 1871)

The daily, early morning trip to town,
To that arctic, ancient church
With devoted ass, shaky cart,
And a barely discernible frown.
A toothful of whisky taken
To ease a gnawing pain
In a taxing molar.
Was she somehow left forsaken?

Fasting from midnight,
Dressed in mourning black
For daily Mass celebrated
To appease the gods
For perceived misdeeds
Or partings from
The obligations of dogmatic theology
And its ill-judged proclamations
That cluttered the minds of the fearful faithful
With white noise
And ill-thought-out, gratuitous declarations.

The daily theatre to be performed—
—Introibo ad altare Dei—*
The principal, in chasuble, stole, and maniple adorned,
The unfolding drama,
Interspersed with the bread of life
And the gongs of bells, the rattle of beads, the shuffling feet.
The dead mourned.
And bowed heads in semi-trance,

Corpus Christi,
The *Deo gratias* response.
And on special days and in special ways,
The granting of plenary indulgences
From Rome—
Wiping the slate clean
Of permanent and temporary stains,
Residues of imagined transgressions,
And gratuitous obsessions—
Keen
To prey upon the meekest minds, seeking to attain
Some vague acquaintance with what might have been.

In the morning stillness she remains, in part obsessed,
Until the concluding words are said
And the final genuflections made:
Et verbum caro factum est.**

The patient beast still waits and waits
For formal orders to complete the daily grind,
Then pitter-patters homewards to her restive foal,
And thereby validates the imprinted instincts of her kind.

Thank you, Granny, for the train and track
And the hours of joyous fun lying on my back
On uneven floors
In a song-filled house
Replete with love
For a red-haired, freckle-faced, timorous child.

*I will go on to the altar of God
**And the word was made flesh.

A Memory

Sweet dates, the exotic produce of Arab states,
Lie seductively on her kitchen table.
I'm going home now,
And I won't be coming back
Until tomorrow, when the horse is to be shod,
The hooves pared,
And I'm given the nod
By her who must be obeyed
To appropriate the delicious fruit of Arab states.

A Hibernian Holocaust,

1845

We, too, are holocaust survivors,
Victims of wayward, corrupt governance.
Famished, tarnished souls
Paying iniquitous tithes
For political expediency.
The landowning, self-serving law enforcers,
Upholders of tendentious law,
The Whiggish nightmare,
The laissez faire business plans
Evicted famished tenants from their homes and
Wasted farms worked by arthritic hands.
The staple crop destroyed by
Rampant deadly *Phytophthora infestans*.
Withered leaves and blackened tubers
Feeding the Grim Reaper
That mercilessly stalked our lands.

Sunday Break:

Sunday Miscellany

Truth is, we take an hour out from our week
To listen to creative energy
Dispensed through the airways
By the 'magic' of technology,
Electromagnetic radiation,
Moving fast,
—The speed of light—
Bringing respite for those who seek
Stories, poems, and happy tales,
That break the monotony of the week.

Anzac Day,

Hamilton, New Zealand, Six a.m., 25/4/2015

A premature start.
It's dark, and a pre-emptive autumn chill pervades the scene.
I witness a gathering—
Music,
Speeches,
Proud old dudes in blazers adorned
With medals,
Young guys representing departed heroes
Casually mown down in Anzac Cove.
Another Churchillian folly,
Mere cannon fodder
Mobilised to stop the Turkish bullets.
Churchill's mug is missing,
But the Anzacs were dutifully there.
Heaven knows why
They travelled, despite their pressing cares,
From distant lands to die
For a cause that wasn't theirs.

Flamingos Feeding,

San Pedro del Pinatar, Summer 2015

Under a candid azure sky,
I perceived a shimmering sea
Mirroring the cloudless firmament,
Bounded in part by concrete emptiness to the East.
Whilst close by, a solitary cagey, pink flamingo
Ponderously goose-steps her zigzag way
To a richer crustacean-laden feeding-ground to feast
On titbit delicacies nourished by black-grey muds and more
Deposited by aeons of geological activity
At the bottom of the densely briny Mar Menor.

Going to the Pump,

Clifden, Clara, County Kilkenny 1958

From a mother's calm voice set
A challenging chore for a child,
Especially in chilly, chafing winds.
She's given him a wide berth
To traipse to the pump for wayward water,
That precious, hard, and sticky blood of our ancient
Primal earth.
Heavy pump-handle lifted—
Steady, steady, at an even pace—
Then pressure dropped
To draw and squeeze the priceless liquid from its hidden home
In the prehistoric, limestone caverns of our place.
It gushed and gurgled noisily
With each succeeding stroke,
Making discordant orchestral sounds—
A rhythmical drumbeat—
On the bottom of the banged-up enamelled bucket,
Dinged, chipped, and dented from years of use.

Oh, to have those days again.
To say the things I should have said.
'I love you, Mum.'

On Reading Kavanagh's Poems

While reading Kavanagh's poems
In the late October light,
I reflect
On his rich-textured lines,
Replete with the peals of holy agriculture and the toil of man,
And of divine, priestly sweat on a wrinkled brow,
Reminiscent of childhood awe of the black soutane
And of the shiny clay left behind the now almost-silent horse-drawn plough.
They remind me, too, of the father's uneven trudges in the freshly opened earth,
The slithery worms, the demanding birds.
All of these
In the wake of odorous horse urine
And animal sweat
And the swarthy plough
On track,
Adjusted by the expert eye
To open the sod, to herald a new spring,
To bring new life back.

'Grand stretch in the evenin's, Jack?'
'Aye, thank God.'
'Hubauf there Nan,' came the voice at the headland.
'Eeeeasy now.'
A light rain falls gently on the fresh, pale-coloured earth.
The light fades;
It's time to go home.

The Bomb,
Los Alamos, Autumn 1941

The fulsome face of fission
Appears in a dark-grey mushroom cloud
Built in the sparse New Mexico desert
On a lunar landscape without conscience.
Conventional war is now redundant,
As thousands in Hiroshima
Died in vain
And humanity cried.

A war crime of immense proportions
Is perpetrated.
The deeply troubled Oppenheimer descends into
The pits of hopelessness.
The revenge of Strauss,
Part of the communist conspiracy!
Un-American activities,
A security risk,
To the arrogance on stilts
Establishment.
Bugs buried deep in his bread bin,
The kangaroo court followed on—
A broken man, a traitor, a man of sin.

A built legacy of radioactivity
To scar the face of the human conscience
Forever.
I have become death, the destroyer of worlds.

The Death of Cleopatra

Defeated by Octavius,
Anthony departed by his own hand.
The sacred one plans her exit
By an infusion of holy asp venom
Into her hallowed breast
To go gently into that good night.
The deadly snake deployed
To inoculate her Hapsburg-like
Incestuous blood, thereby
Pledging and assuring eternal happiness.

The venomous snakes smuggled past the guards
In a basket of sun-ripe figs.
The triumphant Romans rampant,
She couldn't go on.
Nor could she face the humiliation
Of being flaunted through the streets of Rome
By the enemy,
Like a southern harlot
Getting her due desserts,
Thereby validating the pre-eminence
Of the enemy's gods.

A Safe Pair of Hands

Structured language fails again, and logic carelessly cast away.
He didn't share their beliefs.
He didn't conform to irrational dogma.
He wasn't highly regarded.
He was outside the fold.
He was of the view that teaching dogmatic tenets to the child
As 'unalterable truths' distressing.
His story was never fully told,
Always mendaciously distorted.
And he wasn't appointed.
The holy one, supported by the civil arm,
Didn't short-list him.
Hands were not safe enough, would do too much harm.
Ah, but times have changed!
Tacit atheists in the Dáil now;
Politically correct casuistry is easier there.
Equal opportunity goes awry.
The ethos resonates
With my town of earlier times:
Roman Catholics need not apply.

The Willy Week,
2016

Young and old,
Sitting at the feet of the battle-hardened masters,
Swarming 'round honey pots of sweet, rhythmical music—some with
Flutes,
Some with fiddles,
And others with pipes,
And boxes—
Making joyous, harmonic sounds.
Jigs, reels, hornpipes, mazurkas, and slides,
Joyous faces, technical expertise
Demonstrated
Boundless possibilities,
Mick and Rick.

Life and Death:

Tempus Fugit

Life is so full
Of bereavements
And partings.
The pain of separation
Grinds my teeth
And fills my tear ducts
With brackish water.

The Endgame

While listening to one of Chopin's etudes,
He realised that life is short.
The endgame is now.
Now, yes.
Our time is short;
Our time is always too little.
We have no control over the Grim Reaper.
He is a wily fellow, it seems.
Elusive and deadly,
He'd awaken the devil from his dreams.

Drones:

Weapons of Death

(For Jay)

A distressing murderous device
Prowls, shadows, and menaces our world.
Lurking instruments of loss, sulky drones.
Technologically tainted testaments to barbarity,
There's to be no due process for the citizen
Taken out from where he stands
Without recourse.
This sinister technology of death
Stalks the land—our world—and
With pinpoint accuracy,
This disturbing monster
Annihilates its target.
There is no recourse
To the judge
Or
To the eleven equals to articulate
The sentence.

The drone is the judge.
The drone is the jury.
The drone is the executioner.
The silence is eternal.
The dreams and promises of July 4, 1776,
Thwarted, heads turned.

The precious rights to
Life, liberty,
And the pursuit of happiness
Spurned.

The weaponised terrorist reigns supreme.

Fear

Addiction …

I was long afraid
That they'd find out
My troubling penchant
For drinking stout

Was keeping me awake
Until the dead of night.
And then I'd scream
And curl up tight.

Belief …

I also feared
The wrath of God
For not believing
In the Decalogue.

Failure …

I played a match
In the dark, dark night,
Going for goal,
The angle tight.

Avoiding study in the study hall …

Skimming a book
Underneath my desk,
In place of Virgil
Or the less grotesque.

Worries …

Sometimes, too,
I'd stir at night,
Drenched in sweat
And full of fright.

An address to make,
Sweat glands unlock,
A nervous twitch,
Impedes the talk.

Losing a toddler …

She wandered off,
Did not keep up.
We worried intensely for
Our buttercup.

Out West:
Loop Head

And sometimes too
We'd head out West
And take large draughts
Of the setting sun.

And then we'd wander
About the Loop
Till darkness lands
To take us home.

Bells:

Striking a Blow for Civil Liberties

The church bells
Chimed a doleful tune,
De profundis.
Psalm 130,
Chanted in graceful time, in Latin,
At high noon.

Another terrorised soul
Departing early to face his God;
Judgement impartial, death final,
And the iron rod
Applied, intensified.
A coterie of priests
Troop around the catafalque,
Sprinkling holy water
On the seasoned oak,
Dank vapours mixing with some potent incense
And rich, grey-black, charcoal smoke.

Lines of sobbing faithful
Occupy the foremost pews,
'Sorry for your troubles
And the terrible news.
He was a brave man,
Heroically fought
For a noble cause,
The cause of freedom,
From unjust laws.'

Shot dead by British soldiers.
Caught in the act
Underneath a car.
It was his solution—
His endeavour—
Trying to re-ignite,
A failed and faltering revolution.

Tricolour-clad, coffin conveyed
To the waiting hearse
And loaded up.
Yet another blow struck
For civil liberties.

We walked in an ungodly farcical alliance,
In respectful reticence to the grave,
While the grey, unwelcome drizzle
Fell heavily on our silence.

And then the shots rang out.

The Lime Kiln

The seasoned clock clicked and chimed its way through winter
As it had
Without a hint of tedium
For many winters past.
Millennia had elapsed,
Building the fossil-rich limestone bed
Now garnered recklessly from the ancient quarry
And splintered
For making 'burning' easier.
Childhood memories
Of long days,
Of heavy work,
Winged pests,
Muscle tests,
And smelly, sweaty vests.

The blue-grey calcite stone,
Layered with ancient coal,
Calcining,
Deforming,
In the kiln to expel
Those unwanted gases,
The root of global warming.

The days went by.
The temperature rose,
Up to a thousand ranged.
The fire glowed.
The colours changed,
The heat unbearable,

Dantean temperatures at the vent hole;
Air overhead shimmering, terrible.

He couldn't have been prouder:
Soft grey rock
Transmogrified to
White-grey, caustic ash
For sweetening the land,
For coating walls,
For manufacturing steel,
For purifying water,
For destroying evidence.

Lucy

When you're only three,
It's a busy day,
Settling Owlie,
And making tea
In Auckland
For Nana faraway,
In the West of Ireland!

The daily battle—
Getting dressed
With sleepy eyes
And easy, enchanting prattle.

And then there's Ted,
That big fawn dog.
Expectant eyes, gentle ways,
Always ready.

Poet's Track to roam,
By the subtle Waikato's
Dark waters, running deep.
He's loathe to return home.

There's so much fun
Chasing sticks, playing tricks,
And following scents
Down a trampled leaf-strewn run.
And meanwhile, Lucy's playing in the sun.

Ineluctable Conclusions:

Unweaving a Rainbow

(On Visiting Mooghaun, Clare
27 August 2016)

I

The conclusions are inexorable, bold,
Our late-bronze age ancestors' ways exposed
In pollen, stone, and indestructible gold.
One marker simple, elemental;
The others complex, surreal, and cold.
Gold and pollen endure.
Six thousand-year-old stories viewed,
Despite the ravages of time,
To disclose
Ancestral needs for shelter, ornaments, and food.
Ancient ways, some yet untold,
Sophisticated farming practices,
And their acculturated art
Stamped in ornamental gold.

II

They speak to us now
In gold, pollen, bronze, and stone;
Darwin and Attenborough,
Take a gracious bow.

There are patterns sown,
Everywhere quantifiable.
Rich layers and seams
Of thoughts laid down

By those who've gone before,
Waiting to be mined
And analysed.
Infinity and more.

III

Another day
In another place,
A seam emerges.
Mathematics cracks it;
Turing's imaginings
Skirt the verges

And wins the war
Without guns
Or bombs,
But with the purified ore
Of numerical analysis
And three-layer structured hardware
That breaks the enigmatic codes
With sticky algorithms grown
With very little fanfare.
An eponymous legacy confidently thrown

Amongst the seams and threads of life
Unbroken in the ground,
Exposed by a curious man
With a crusty, well-worn coring knife.

IV

Gene by gene,
And tedious base by base,
Ancient legacies exposed,
Allowing us to trace
Our ancestry
Before the window in the door is closed.

Never Count the Dead

(Apologies and grateful thanks to Bob Dylan and Dominic Behan)

Chemical dust,
Radioactive waste,
Loneliness
On the east side of the street.
An empty cup
Collecting pence
From the busy shopper,
While the vacuous thrash on the fence
Acquiesce.

Everything comes crashing down.
It doesn't make sense;
I'm human too,
Tangled up in blue.
Give him the gallows.
He's a traitor;
He betrayed the cause
For music
While grasping at straws.

Mary Frankincense's about.
You wouldn't think
Butter would melt in her mouth.
No, butter wouldn't melt
In the bitch's mouth.

She's a sycophant.
Why should we clean her air?
Why would you treat her fair?
Sick in mind and
Self-obsessed, vigorously taking notes:
Will I lose those marginal, crucial votes?

———•—•———

A child puts up his hand.
'Help me, Miss.
I don't have food.
I need a kiss
And a bottle of milk
From someone who cares.
Take me from this sulphurous abyss.'

———•—•———

Russian rockets
Destroy their homes.
The tyrant's murderous intent
To wipe his tortured people
From the face of Mother Earth.

Damned beast
Partaking in an infernal feast
While his charges die,
And Mary takes her Spanish fly.

The Faith Healer

I can cure you
For fifty euro.
I have this power, this special gift.
Witness Mary's testimony here.
She'll attest
To what is best
About our operation.

It's a set-up; get out of town.

The conjurer,
The illusionist,
Turns a trick
Of pitiless dimensions.

Preying on the beliefs
Of innocent minds and
Charges for mendacities
And empty lies, without a hint of fear or dread,
Building conflated pensions,
While he ties
A mortgage to a villa by the Med.

Spanish Neanderthals

The Cabezo Gordo,
The Sima De Las Palomas,
Quietly holding its secrets
For 300 millennia.
Distinct species,
Hunter-gatherers roaming
The bison-rich, Murcian plain.

Chilly Winds

17/11/2016

From the pitch-black North today,
Sleet-laden winds blow through,
An angry, rising sky
From the deep, grey, black Atlantic.
Saline winds signalling summer's end
And stripping the remaining
Bronzed and brittle leaves
From weather-beaten skeletal trees which bend,
Unaware that the chilly day is late,
That global warming is well advanced
By one degree.

So we wend our merry way,
With fossil-fuelled intoxicated views,
Through a sea of confusion
And denial,
And calmly to the music dance.
Ignoring science
We slink along
The road to perdition,
Imbibing propagandist noise,
Creationist trance,
The great Chinese hoax,
The obfuscator's circumstance.

Mescaline Haze

30/11/2016

Opening an alluring door to deep consciousness,
An alkaloidal miasma,
A peyote cactus extract
Used in sacramental rituals
By the Native American church.
Hallucinogenic power
That changes perception and
Grants a foretaste of eternal happiness
Or Faustian damnation.
A tri-methoxy amine.

Amen.

Sharing Wealth

His litigious excellency,
In defence of human rights,
Goes to court,
The citizens' protection in his sights!
Another unequal money war,
Selling hard-pressed citizens short.

His corporation is now a person
Which can be defamed
But not imprisoned;
Oh, no, that's a step too far!

He owns the airways.
He sacks those he doesn't like.
He's courted by the mighty.
It's daunting to plumb his psyche.

He doesn't pay much tax.
He prefers to choose his charities.
He prefers to adjust disparities
By funding running tracks.

The Deniers

The integrity of authentic science
Inexorably questioned
By the rejuvenated hellish spectre of
McCarthyism.
Debate is polarised,
Assisted by newspaper science,
Management science, fake news
Destroying the fundamentals

Of human thought.
Sensationalism wins.
Data cherry-picked,
Gratuitous assertions, and such kind
Compete with complex scientific data
To inform the unsuspecting mind.

A plague of ads
Distorts our vision and
Climate change exaggerated.
NASA satellites, orbiting the earth every ninety minutes,

Looking down repeatedly,
Collecting
Terabytes of data daily.

Historic temperature changes
Solid.

The planet is warming.
'Listen', she says, 'the planet's warming.'
The rate is accelerating.

Fred Singer, the sceptic,
Deploys gratuitous citations—
Solar wind's to blame.
Data cherry-picked to enhance his name
And attain populist ovations.

The sun is not the primary cause of change;
Seven giga-tonnes per year of CO_2 and growing
Emitted carelessly by man.
Whom do we believe?
Whom do we trust?
Climategate!
A scientific scandal
Used by the naysayers
To destroy
Phil Jones.
Rings in trees 4,000 years old
Make a proclamation.
Peer reviews of station data.
Authentic scientific work
Makes supporting statements.

The irrational sceptics and naysayers
Rely on lies and bogus news;
GM trials disrupted by madmen.
We have the weight of history
On our shoulders.
We mustn't betray the real heroes.
'Remember', she said,
'1660, the first meeting of the Royal Society.'
Trust what the data tell you.
Politicisation of science
Is now commonplace,

The propagandist's weapon
To fool the unwary. Beware!
And remember
The Origin of Species,
And remember
The Principia Mathematica,
'And remember too', she said,
'Sir Paul Nurse'.
We are not
Unweaving Keatsian rainbows.
We weave new ones.'
The billionaires cannot be allowed to win.

Failures

Is it something in our genes
Or environment
That raises fears of trying
Things we should?

It's okay to fail.
It's okay to trail
Behind successful souls.

The Alien One:

Xenon

Not empathic, distant, cold
Asperger's, for which there's no cure,
No bonding with the family
Or outside.
Scheming, calculating, inure

To feeling, inert, alien.
Fluorine-arranged marriage,
Successful interaction,
Possible crisis, potential miscarriage.

Fluorine and platinum persist.
Possible Nobel Prize.
A new compound born,
Under sixties' skies.

It's not a collision of black holes.
Not even a newer planet.
But a brand-new, worthy compound
With newfound values with a novel tenet.

Upsetting the theory
Of inertness,
Of nobility without a crown,
While turning conventional, scientific wisdom
Significantly upside down.

Pandering to Illusions

That's the way it was,
A benchmark for morality.
The practice of the times,
Shredded memories
Of immortality and signs
And signals that

We live on
In our genes and youthful memories.
We die when we succumb
To sycophantic ceremonies.

We perceive
A world of vain illusions
And contrived contusions
Of the last fake battle.
Ah, we're so naïve.

We've had our pain.
We abjure the battle
We cannot win
Against a powerful aristocracy.

We build a wall.
We divide our people
While we're held in thrall
To shameless rogues
Pounding pulpits
In chapels without steeples.

Winter

In the deep, deep pits of winter,
Summer sunshine radiating from the grate,
Fused in firewood garnered
From the landed gentry's ruined estate.

Slanting remnants of sunnier days
Dimly lighting up our northern room.
Frost nails dripping tenuously
From the shimmering, spiny broom.

In the moss-enveloped garden,
The robin scanning gingerly—not a sound—
For maggots that have gone astray
In that frost-hardened, grey, unyielding ground.

The blackbird listens, head askance,
For movements in the soil.
The fieldfare trips and hops perchance
To spy a wayward worm while

Yet again, I garner kindling
For the slow, slow fire.

Getting Over It

The bittersweet,
Digoxin-laden, digitalis flowers
Shed pink prettiness
On the shimmering late-summer water; several hours

Downstream,
Hearts beat faster,
And younger, terrified, romantic people scream
About a perfectly,
Delicious, frenzied, banking disaster,

Denying bricks and mortar
For the shattered homeless young
(So highly strung).
Worried about petty,
Inconsequential,
Trivial matters.

Marble fireplaces
Compete with shiny Porsches,
Indicators of excessive wealth
Whilst neglecting social health.
The man in the duffel coat
Walks in
With dishevelled hair
And an unkempt neckerchief about his throat.

He's a kind of cult person,
A kind of thinker,
Building sandcastles that are wild, insane,
That will ultimately crumble and shatter
In a summer's inundation
Of finely divided rain.

Night Flight

On the elite, exclusive bus to Mars,
The trip is just for those
Who can afford a seat,
But not for those who choose
To reach thoughtfully for the stars.

I can hear that sense of loss
In the plaintive airs
He plays
On those agéd, flattened pipes.
But he won't be on the bus to Mars.

No, he's little,
Like the other petty people.
Hewers and drawers
Who continue
To plant trees
As heaven roars
Its concerns for the future.

The ancient sceach bush
On Freestone Hill
Tells a story
That will
Knock you out
And undermine your
Complacent, baseless repertory.

I can assure you
We're in a trance.
But I can cure you
For fifty euro;
I can make the hopeless dance.

We waltzed around the room today
To Leonard's 'Take This Waltz'.
One pretty woman who could dance,
She did it in her peerless way.

Go Figure:

19 March 2003, Bush and Blair Invade Iraq

Iraq, a wholly autonomous
And independent place,
Its silent, defenceless people—
Maybe unorthodox—
But is that not okay?
Land laid waste by bombs
And bloodthirsty coalition hawks,
A malign, destructive treat,
A Trojan horse
Based on senseless, mindless lies
And malevolent deceit.

The 'liberation' of Iraq,
A cradle of ancient civilisation,
The deliverance of Halliburton,
Defending rightful freedom!

Solid intelligence
Exposes no real threat
Posed by a poor country
Where innocent children die;
Armaments—solid shares set
To soar sky-high.

Fox News
Tells the 'truth'
About the
Killing machines,
The killing fields.

American boys
From American schools'
Coffins could not be seen.
Too upsetting, so wrong
For the unresponsive dupes
Thoughtlessly recruited to ensure
That the exploiters' shares remain resiliently strong.
The combat zone is
Making friends down the barrel of a gun.
Ah, yes,
Santa Claus is comin' to town.

The Christmas Cake

Made with love
And care,
She takes time out
To share

An open tin for a sweet tooth.
The whiff of
Brandy
And delicious fruit

Speak the truth
About the world
Of childhood memories—
Uncomplicated, unfurled.

The Proclamation Remembered

2016

Steady hands are needed now
To aver or rebut a doubtful, fragile freedom,
Hitherto undefined in meaning.
It's far, far too soon yet
For a triumphant
And glorious *Te Deum*.

Freedom from sin
And deprivation,
Freedom to maim
And instigate salvation.

Freedom to punish,
Freedom to prefer
Friends to enemies
With gifts, and then confer
Appointments well-deserved—
Though nothing to inspire us—
On those who helped
Remove the age-old, foreign virus.

It's a phantom
Chased by fools from caves,
Who believe the sycophantic hoopla
Of hothouse-tutored knaves.

We succumb
To sham news and promises.
We abjure our capacity to think.
We carelessly trust untested hypotheses.

The National Debt Revisited:
That Special Purpose Vehicle

Furtive schemes were formed in frenzied secret cultures
Flouting hard-won citizens' rights,
While our hard-earned silver's seized
By opportunistic, unconscionable vultures.

Sixty billion of debt attached
To a debt-ridden, muted citizen.
Secret deals were hatched
Outlandishly and preposterously political.

While in the very safest hands,
Bets were honoured at the starting price,
All wagers well respected
In our rapacious investors' paradise.

It's not too much to expect
That bankers do a well-paid job
And show a smidgen of respect
For those of us they rob.

Our respected minister's stumped.
Harvard attorneys ascend the stairs
In pinstripe, well-pressed suits
And pseudo-sophisticated airs.

Now that's the special purpose vehicle.
That's the Henry VIII despotic clause,
Another moronic executive order
Exploited furtively to sustain
A disturbingly, antisocial cause.

Another bloodless coup
Seamlessly executed.

Pain

Some days there's pain
That's short and sharp.
Some more extended, in the brain.
If I kneel and pray,
It goes away,
Though the pain of loss and separation
Leaves an indelible and enduring stain.

Early Spring Flowers:

A Confederacy of Dunces

Just one furze flower
Peeps furtively from behind
A frost-covered
Faraday cage.

It's been said
We're blind
To the frequent changes
Emanating
From behind
Those fog-covered mountain ranges.

The female moose looks fretful
For her calf,
While a white-haired demagogue
Is unaware, unaware by half,
Of what is going on.

The blackbird's busy,
And the crocus's early.
Listen here,
They know something's up
When winter frosts prematurely
Disappear.

Authentic science and attendant tools
Are undermined
By an unholy alliance
Of a confederacy of dunces and
Of wayward, licensed fools.

The End of Music

The time has come,
The time is now, to realise
That somehow cherry blossoms
Survive the enduring winter's snow
In the womb of the embryonic bud.

The deep symphonic score
Programmed over very many hours
Is secreted in the genes
And is then orchestrated
In the silk-like, sterile flowers,

That form a carpet
Of petals on the ground
To amuse
And sensuously astound
The drifting passer-by.

What evolutionary path did the sterile cherry take
To scatter its riches
Far and wide and leave within its wake
A worrying puzzle for reflective evolutionists?

On a Trip to Abu Dhabi

30/01/2017

A troubled world vibrates below
With atrocities committed by the hour.
Baghdad out there to the West—
It's 14.00 Irish—as the Syrian people cower.

One hour or so to go
And then we land at Abu Dhabi
From Dublin on a fuel-consuming
Monster of technology,
The Boeing 777-300.

Another monster kills his people way below.
He calls them terrorists.
And he should know:
The strongest always wins

And writes the history
With ink of blood
On parchment
Made from children's hides
In many a devastated
And embattled neighbourhood.
As the vermillion sun sinks
Slowly and ponderously
In the West
While children scream.

Visits to the mosque will recompense
The tyrant who says, 'No, no,
The Qur'an now makes sense.
I am an earthly god sent,
So listen and repent.

I am the other Ozymandias.'

DJ: Hurling Wizard

(for Martin)

In less troubled spaces,
DJ takes the oily ball in the wet
And weaves his way seamlessly
Towards the goal,
Rattling the back of the opponent's net.

Oh, to have those days again,
To watch a hurling wizard work,
Ignoring game-induced, persistent pain
With sliotar on hurley
Stuck.

Adept and devastating footwork
And hands
With well-made plans
To split the posts
In the opponent's goal.

A flick of the wrist could be shattering.

Gödel's Theorem

Two and two make four;
It just makes perfect sense.
But Kurt Gödel
Did not sit unobtrusively
On that over-crowded fence.

Within the formal system
There are statements that make sense
Which cannot be proved
Or disproved, however deep the penetration

Of the analysing mind,
However prejudiced
It may seem to
Fully evolved mankind.

The E Major Chord

There's that inner voice,
The excitement
That emerges
When I hear that tune.
It appears with C major
And C minor
In Beethoven's "Diabelli Variations"
And lightens the strength
Of the entire piece,
And eases the pain of life.

The Man with the Beard in Café 9:

A Poem for Vengseng

(Otherwise Wayne)

He came in again today,
Grabs the *Times*.
Sweat-stained hat he sets aside,
Exposing a shock of long, greying, tangled hair.
This is his way

To relax.
Not a single word.
He drinks a strong, black coffee.
It feels so utterly absurd.

I await a greeting,
Or something with some feeling.
But I wait and wait.
He's staring, staring, staring without seeing.

They say he's a mountainy man
From Maunganui,
Exterminating imported pests
That threaten the noisy tui.

He has that look,
That gimp of loneliness,
Inarticulate,
Quiet,
Deep.

Setting diphacinone at the boss's behest,
And sometimes deadly cyanide,
Attempting to turn the relentless tide
On an invasive, furry, foreign pest.

Without a word—I can assure you,
Even without a knowing glance—
He grabs his hat and furtively
Sets his face towards Rotorua.

Moments of Reprieve:

I Make No Hypotheses

The persecution of Galileo meant
That science became Protestant.
Italy was left behind
In science and industry, and
Newton, the unloved man—
Solitary, deep—
Inventing fluxions,
Universal gravitation,
Reciprocal of squares,
Lunar period
Twenty-seven-point-two-five days.

And elliptical paths,
Action at a distance,
A scientific method landmark.
1666 the glass prism
Splitting light,
Unweaving the rainbow.

Labels

The shocking truth is
You're a nerd.
Hyperactive,
Outside the herd,
Twitching, twitching, twitching.

The man in the suit and tie
Paid a visit here today
To cast aspersions and cast his eye
And earn his public-service pay

For classifying us
With Tourette's
Or worse.
But I was just
Pretending.

Heard Haldol mentioned.
This could be life-changing.
Tic, Tic, Tic.

Hobbes, Hugo, and Hume

Their works were banned
From the native's reading list
To protect the curious apprentice
From sober, dry, intellectual grist.

The expert drafters,
From their ivory towers,
Ruled these inventors out
To protect the citizen
For fear that there'd be afters

In the corridors of power.

The Ohakune Train

Mount Ruapehu, laced with lazy snow,
Inspired intrepid settlers
With pick and hoe
As they transmogrified the gorges.

They cut the native trees and brought the track
To wild and desolate places,
Where no rational elements of the human race
Should ever set their hardened faces.

Shifting stumps of ancient, long-limbed Rimu,
Laying Romanesque-like cobbled roads
For horse-drawn, creaky carriages
Between the Horopito and the Ohakuné nodes.

From Tuamarunui
To Ohakuné,
Gateway to the Tongariro Mountain pass,
A world of crystal glacier melt,
Clear as a looking glass.

Early Autumn Bush Sounds:

Te Awamutu, Waikato, NZ, 7 March 2017

The chirping woodland birds,
The ceaseless, never-ending,
High-pitched screech
Of cycads, declaring their gene-driven needs,
Light up the bush
With cheerful sounds,
While the white yarrow flower
Quietly, so unobtrusively,
Forms its seeds
In readiness.
Close by, the buttressed pukatea
Vies with the lanky kahikatea
In their ancient, swampy home
For life-giving sustenance.

Above the din, the tui sings.
The bellbird rings
His doleful bell
To warn of the new arrivals.

Away, away.
I can hear the tui now
As he flutters furtively from tree to tree
And sings his melodious tune
High up in a leaf-dark canopy.

A Hidden Legacy

On the building down the street,
The Virgin's statue
And the crucifix can still be seen,
Declaring to the world
The power and fortitude
Of an unpretentious Nazarene.

I quietly perceive the furtive whispers
Of the 1950s 'round our place,
Where the selfless holy sisters
Led a virtuous and worthy race
To save and protect us at whatever cost
From fallen, brazen hussies
Just in case
Another unblessed soul is lost.

Here the nameless men don't care.
They just walk away to attend their station,
Leaving their hapless offspring there
To face needless cruelty, pain, and undying desperation.

Cruelty is virtuous.
Unblessed procreation is a vice
For which untutored, unloved women
Paid a hellishly inordinate price

For departing from
The herd,
For vindicating a female urge
To procreate

And seal her fate,
And thereby purge
Society of a savage threat.

A holy house of horrors
In a sacred place.

Forgotten:

The Holy Innocents Reborn

Often have I wondered what it's like
To bear a child for the Roman reich,
And then to part with a treasure born
Without a name
For export in which we all collude
As the mother's held in scorn
By the long-subverted multitude.

On a Train to Bournemouth

Spring has landed.
At last the hoary blackthorn blossoms
Whiten the unadorned land,
Competing with mustard furze
For the rapt attention
Of early, errant bees.

A Royal Entitlement

That famous house had kept its secrets
In spite of a tendentious and brutal law.
The mistress was protected
By her royal, sheltered fingertips—
Being held in fearsome awe—
From the merciless and brutal transport ships.

She escaped the fate that befell her sisters
In far off van-Diemen's Land
In Sydney Harbour, in Botany Bay's dead hand,
And in the Norfolk Island ditches.
She was spared
The fatal shore.

Those transported
Suffered a gestapo horror,
Desperate, lost.
But the motherland
Was incapable of any
Hellish, pitiless Holocaust!

There were no ovens,
There,
Nor prussic acid,
No synthetic Zyclon-B.
Just a slower death,
By decree,
In chains.
Brutal, unending sweat,
And constant, incessant pains.

And when I naively enquire,
He smiles,
He stares.
Is it not thus we build an empire?

Powerlessness

She entered there
In trust for care
To see her newborn
Through those perilous days.

The baby came,
Relief at last.
But alas, would have no name from Rome
But that conferred in foster care
In an American, Roman Catholic home.

Nature never wished,
As nature never does,
To consign the innocent
In the full flush

Of life
To interminable damnation,
To finger-pointing whispers
Serving self-righteous roles
Enough to crush
The sturdiest of souls.

Here Comes the Sun

(For Lucy)

Here comes the sun,
My beautiful one.
It's way past seven.
There's lots
To be done.
No time to stare
While painting with Nana,
Eating tasty, melty eggs
And a sun-filled, juicy pear.
So when we're through,
We'll pick spring flowers
And talk about busy robins
Bobbing here and there
In Grandad's event-filled garden.

Wasted on Margaritas in Dublin, Early Sixties

She bumped her ample bosom
Across my bleedin' desk.
She lacerated me so eloquently
For stuff so wildly, mad, grotesque
I couldn't possibly ever fix.

Her little boy had been
So neglected.
Had I no damn control?
Had I no bleedin', anxious, fearful soul?

'Ah! Jaysus mam,
You're too severe,
I'm just implementing absurd rules
Set by dull officials
Acting in a dumb, official sphere.'

'A Jaysus mam,' again.
'You don't seem to have a clue
About the mind-numbing
Rules established by that idiotic,
Subservient, Marlboro crew.

That's a street in Dublin, mam,
Called after a famous military man, and
Not that far from Dolphin's Barn.

We must follow
The Holy Qur'an,

Or is it the Bible, mam?

I just don't know anymore
Which sacred book
From which we can
Implore, appeal, and
Obtain our guiding rule.

No, you don't understand.
I wasn't good at school
But played me cards
And kept the rule
And got where I am.
So cooool.'
'I knew it', she said,
'Another damn crustacean,
Another genuflecting fool
Above his station.
Hard to believe
The product of an ancient, noble nation.'

'Yes,' I said to Johnny—
That's my husband,
You understand.
I said, 'That school's
No good; we need to lend a helping hand
And move our fretful child to another brand
Of sweet indoctrination.'

'Ah there's nothing we can do.
No, nothing.
How can a mere trawneen
Upset that massive, fuming didgeridoo?'

Sotto voce
'I'm a closet anarchist, mam.
You must get out of here.
Look at my tangled hair,
The beard,
And all the trappings of despair.'

'There's no art to find the mind's constriction
In the face,' she says.

'Ah Jaysus, it's construction.
Do you hear me, "it's construction"?
Get it right for God's sake.'

No harm.

'Oh, my sweet sufferin' Jaysus, he's mad.
And I'm from Dolphin's Barn.'

Fulfilment of a Dream:

October Sky, aka Rocket Boys

They built their schoolboy rockets
In a damp, dank, darkened shed,
Staying late,
Eschewing bed.

Saltpetre,
Flowers of sulphur,
And finely divided carbon black
As they create a stink, a bang, and many's the frown.
There was to be no looking back
For those boys
From that bustling West Virginia mining town.

Science, Religion and Urban Myths

on the Wild Atlantic Way

I walked past that corroded, rusty sea gate
On a Wednesday afternoon.
The roaring tide
Left me speechless
And with very little wiggle room.

For original brazen thought
Is sparse, thin, and bare,
And has been since
Cambrensis's day,
Or since Bishop Berkeley
Had his say.

We are conflicted with specious thoughts
And the superior thinking of the foe.
The Irish were barbaric savages,
Full of erroneous beliefs,
Full of doleful woe.

And then
Cromwell came,
Then William marchèd down.
We were mere bloody cannon fodder
For a troubled, greedy Crown.

Alan Kurdi:

A Small Boy Cries Out in Silence

(A poem for Alfie Silcock)

The foreseeable consequences
Of a merciless and xenophobic war,
Assign a small boy
To a pasty, dampened, Turkish shore.
He lies forlorn, red T-shirted,
On a lonely strand.
On his face, no cry, a babe asleep.
Boat-slipped from his father's helpless hand
As his parents wail and weep.

His little body motionless—numb—
Brought ashore by a giant wave.
How a baby cry would help us all.
But he shall not now smell the roses on his grave.

Nor shall he know the joy of maths or space
Or science or measured poems,
Or the vast intellectual achievements of his race.
What are those brazen kleptocrats about?
Do they fear their Maker, do they have any nagging doubt?

Or are governance beliefs
Some cynical manipulation
Of gullible believers in divisive prophets,

While innocence is robbed by unbridled thieves?
Innocents displaced scream to God for help
As shrapnel still makes gaping holes in tired roof soffits.

A Turkish soldier carries him away,
And I can feel his numbing pain.
He hopes that
He shall never face
The likes of this again.

Family Matters

He came to me from nowhere
While I fixed my family tree.
He came to me from over there
On his way to Inishfree

Or Ben Bulben Head
Or Knocknarea,
Where Maeve lies fast asleep,
Waiting for a better day
To dawn and set her free
To make meaningful decisions
'bout her doubtful DNA.

Ah, but now
The genie's out;
The sequencing has begun.
We may start to kill the hopeless
And end up like Genghis Khan.

We have the power
To edit genes,
To end the dreams
Of those who've gone before.
We have succumbed to the
Wiles of a reckless, undiscerning whore.

Travails

Sometime in the dim and distant past
I heard some cattle lowing on the hill,
And I perceived a man-made, grey, stone wall
Built thoughtfully to last
To thrill,

To keep the cattle in.
To allow the harsh winds through
To keep intruders out,
Cemented by some ancient, ritualistic,
Priestly, godless, voodoo.

The Entropy Class

'What's entropy,' the master asked.
'Who gives a Friar Tuck?' *sotto voce*.
I heard that as I passed
The open door,
While thinking deeply on what he says.
And then there are times I see my peerless self
As shiny as a convent floor.

'It's something that increases
All the time, sir.
It can't ever be controlled,'
Said someone from a distant threshold
Adjacent to that open door

Of knowledge, deep and fine,
Of scientific bent.
A fruitful sign
Of a future anxious to ferment

Thoughts of theses,
Of necessary truths,
Of random useless thoughts
Of men in suits.

Removing the Filters

The Mozart Clarinet Quintet,
Incomparable eclectic music.
And the Clapton
Guitar, likewise.
Varied tastes
Abound,
Filters removed,
Opening our vacant minds
To excitingly new experiences and exquisite variegated sounds.

We fail on all sorts of fronts.
We fail to see the others'
Points of view.
Ah, narcissism
Takes hold,
Rejecting what is new.

A Sunday Morning Dawdle:
Café con Leche in Torre de la Horadada

I could smell the ardent smoke
Of burning almond wood—
A rose by any other name—
While I stood in the early morning rain.

Industrious trees, wondrous nuts
Replete with goodness,
Unsaturated oils,
And alkaline-earth lees
Garnered spoils
From black-barked, skeletal trees
Nurtured in the fertile soils
Of the historic realm of Andalucía.

He sits across.
I know he works the fields,
All muscle and ink
With sweaty bandana;
Maybe once pink,
I think.

Or red,
The colour of his politics
Now long since dead.

His engagement with his woman is intense.
He stares; there's a lot at stake.
His hands move
To underline a point
He tries so eagerly to make.

Is she a fallen woman?
Ah, that's old hat now.
But why is she not smiling?
Why so many beads of sweat upon her brow?

But while I eavesdrop
And try to listen to what they say,
Abruptly, while I sup
Yet another reckless cup,
He thumps the bench and walks away.

Terezin, Destination:

Auschwitz-Birkenau

This transit space,
For Maria Teresía named,
An unnerving, spiteful place
Wrought by a tyrant to house the Jews
Away from the stresses and soul-destroying strife
And the wearisome strains of life.
And mounds of shoes
And glasses,
Once fondly worn, cared for,
Can still be seen

In the Little Fortress,
In this ghost-ridden,
Fearful place.
The orchestra played the *Ninth*
With incongruously triumphant wind and strings.
The children painted scenes
And played with homemade childhood things.
Homely and unpretentious themes,
Matters seemed quite routine, humane.
When the blinkered Red Cross came

And went, the elderly guided to the ovens,
Fated and doomed to die.
No fervent cry for justice to the heavens.
Just an empty soubriquet
Arbeit Macht Frei.

Atrociously.

Late Breakfast

There's someone having breakfast.
I can hear the scraping of a plate.
Or is it lunch?
Or maybe everything's just running late.

Yes, but not everything is late.
The daffodils bloom in November,
The crocuses appear in December.
The ice melts deep.

There's talk of rising water.
There's talk of destructive waves,
Of forest fires,
Of finding safety in high-up caves.

The swallows are confused.
They don't know when to come or go.
I see them swooping now,
While we await the winter snow.

Union Station, Kansas City,
November 2017

She was seated in a corner
With her unobtrusive, private thoughts
Mixed with coffee and fur-lined gloves,
Joining all the strife-filled dots.
High-ceilinged station
Reverberating with discordant sound
And warmed by fuel-filled stoves,
And the clanks of busy, raucous trains
Underground.

Thrilled by tested science,
By ancient mummies,
And the whispers
And the rattles
Of the every day
At play.

She makes some furtive glances.
'Where to now?'
She seemed to say.

While a street car comes and goes
Every hour—
Twenty minutes
To the river,
Twenty minutes back—
Comfort for the weary,
Shelter for the frozen,

Respite for the slack.
Memories of the wagon trails,
Of famished settlers,
Of wanton waste;
She forgets the squalid details.

Rusty love locks bound to tired fences,
Symbols of eternal love.
Couples forever bonded,
Witnessed solely by the skies above.

The Woman on the 229 Bus,

Kansas City, 13 November 2017

I could see it in her wrinkled face,
The lifelong ravages of addictive nicotine.
The audible wheeze, the shortness of breath,
And other signs that can't be seen.

Impatiently sitting on her seat,
Rocking ceaselessly back and forth,
Heading to her menial job,
A hopeless zero-hour,
Low-paid contract
Near that busy gleaming airport.

Alighting from the bus,
Fag dangling from her mouth
Ready for ignition,
Trembling hand,
Lighter fired,
Ahhhh.
The smoke is going south.
Emphysema vicariously planned.

God, Guns, and Paranoia

In God we trust.
He guides our haughty hand
To a unique brand of mythical exclusiveness.

It's part of the divine plan
To make America great again
With God on our side, no doubt
To commend our nuclear arms
And keep the non-believers out.

In a cold train carriage
I read the news that
Everything is going sour:
Satan is behind same-sex marriage;
Islam is a wicked faith,
Infiltrating the corridors of power.
But Babylon is great.
The whore is dressed in gold.
She rides the savage beast,
While the god of mammon
Hosts a lavish feast.
Meanwhile, the poet labours
Over an incisive, discerning line,
And scrutinises delicate and perfect fines
Filtered through the complex mesh of time.

Making Hay:

Kilkieran, Ballyfoyle, County Kilkenny, June 1955

In Mantan's Field,
That slopes slightly towards the gurgling, grudging stream,
The hay is mown
While barefooted children giggle, dart,
And scream.

The sun is at its zenith
In the vivid, clear-blue, southern sky.
The experienced cut the headlands
With a well-worn, stone-edged scythe.*

'We'll turn it in the morning
And make the grass cocks up by noon.'
We hadn't yet heard
Of any adverse weather warning

That should curb our enthusiasm
For the business left in hand.
So we won't have to pay in winter frosts
A conflated king's ransom.

Horses yoked,
Slide attached,
Hay garnered into rays,
Horses matched;
The driver knows their ways.

Horses tied
Whilst we make the cocks.
Heads shaking,
Legs stamping,
Flies irritating,
Skin twitching,
Tail flailing,
One leg resting.

*Pronounced 'sigh' as in the west of Ireland and elsewhere.

Rock Salt

Taking the plunge into deep darkness,
We'll have no more of it.
No, no it's far too much.
It's a dangerous pit.
But why?
The darkness falls, for God's sake.
We've had our time.
We've had our stake
In global charming.
Happy pills will keep us sane,
Will bring us through gloom-filled days
By anaesthetising the addled brain.

Obsessed by sin
And sanctifying grace,
So befuddled by mundane daily strife.
Obsessed by a sense of place
And the burdensome trivialities of life.

Chavs:
The Undeserving Poor

The deserving, working hoi polloi,
Like the undeserving poor,
Fuel groundless, official fury,
And baseless demonizing
Of the long-suffering deprived doer.

Living comfortably on Benefits' Street,
Like an over-privileged Prince,
Another *Cri de Coeur*,
Another casual, inane rejection
From a bungling leader's seat.

We don't care who pays the bills.
We sidestep the bigger picture
We rely surreptitiously
On the all-pervasive greasy tills.

There's no money
For alleviating pain.
There's just small change for nuclear arms,
From which there is no vicarious human gain.

Take heed, wake up,
We're running out of time.
The valley is deep, we're full of woe;
There's a mountain to climb.
Give up voting for your foe.

It's Not Dark Yet

It's hard to start today.
The sun shines through the window facing south.
The air outside is calm.
I now have thoughts
I cannot say.

Dried up,
Barren,
Block,
Calm.

Seeking Patterns

Sacrificing that fattened goat
Can reassure us that abundant rain
Will soak the ground
To green the grass
To nourish famished cattle once again.

It's happened so many times before.
It happens each and every season.
Our beliefs are exceedingly strong,
Stubbornly withstanding the awkward tests of reason.

Scientific method waits
To extract a counter case
From dogged, persistent patterns
To undermine our flaky space.

Of, 'That's how it's always been,'
Our expectations rarely change.
We depend on sensory traits
To reinforce our unfounded database.

An Old Man:

An Emigrant

I saw him shunting purposefully down a crowd-filled city street.
Painful movements,
Needing help,
He had never learned to tweet.
'I've had my day.
I've had my say.
I never really learned to pray,'
He mutters.
He stands, he gawps
With Zimmer-frame support.
Shakes his fist with a deep sigh.
He smiles and stares
But not one retort
From the harried passer-by.

I knew him in his younger days,
When he laid bareback bricks
With perfect hands in perfect rows,
And mixed mortar by the tonne.
He wasn't fazed by arduous work,
But now his race is almost run.

Gnarled hands,
Arthritic toes
Are the legacies
Of wet, cold,
Winter stands.

Distant days in London haunt him now,
Filling mortar in the tubes,
Paying subbies,
Eating soup
Warmed in coal-fired braziers,
And winnings on the pools.

Backing horses,
Waiting in the cold.
Waiting, waiting
Until the malodorous taverns open
Where he can regale the patrons
With stories yet untold
Of Connemara,
Of small-farm lore,
Of storms, of snow,
Of stories from a love-filled home.

An Army Vet Runs for Congress

He's white.
He looks so swell.
He fought in 'Nam
And in stout Iraq as well.

He's privileged and humbled.
He had nothing at all to gain.
He took down terrorists in Afghanistan.
The swamp needs to drain.
America's under attack
From without,
From within,
He's endorsed by the NRA
And the National Right to Life.
He stands by the Little Sisters.
Alarmingly, gun deaths are rife,
And nuclear arms proliferate
To protect our freedoms
And to build up credit for the afterlife.

An Evening of Ale and Rashers

(For Seamus, a friend of fifty-one years)

Some speak authoritatively on poetry and prose,
Of writers with gifts to dazzle
The stiffest sniffy nose.

Ah, Kavanagh was the man.
And the poet Hartnett too.
Both infused with an understanding
Of that cultured, rustic hue.

Exposing the inner core of being,
Exposing a uniquely Celtic strand
With lines that dazzle the most truculent of minds.
So many look without perceiving

The rich texture of peasant life.
The seams of gold in smells and sounds
Of a May meadow, of a cabin full of cows
On a fog-filled, frosty night.

Something stirs.
The dog barks.
The baby screams.
Grandad farts.

He's nervous now.
His friend is gone.
Death looms large.
The friend, he loved a song

By Chris, by Leonard,
Or by John.

The genius of the chords,
The unanticipated note,
The surprising riff.
Ah, he's dead now.
He's gone.
He's lying on his back.
He's stiff.
And no amount of tears
Will ever bring him back.

I never introduced him to Prine,
To Lake Marie,
To the hole in Daddy's Arm,
The Speed.
He'd have loved that stuff.
We didn't talk enough.
There was so much left to say.

The Regina Coeli was awesome.
The Panis Angelicus,
The Plain Chant.
Ah! Hello in There,
On a Magnolia Wind,
Busted Flat,
My friend.
Goodbye, goodbye, goodbye.

The Corpulent Canon

'Hello boys', he says as he waddles down the study room.
'I expect that you'll be sitting those pesky state exams sometime pretty soon.'
Amo, amas, amat.
'It'll be bedtime with the bell.'
Amamus, amatis, amant.
'So sort yourselves, pack up the books.
Be up in time for Mass,
Or you'll all end up in hell.'

He always laughed out loud.
His balding head,
His flabby gait,
Of his sacred vocation though,
He was immensely proud.

Teaching was his thing.
He could make the stones do maths
And Latin too.

'And by the way, before ye sleep,
Reflect on Aristotle's thought
(Or was it Pliny's?):
Ex Africa semper aliquid novi.
And may the good Lord keep you safe.'

Slings and Guns

Shots ring out daily.
Music breaks through on
Broken radios,
Crackling.
He prepares a sling
Loaded.
No match
For an AK-47
The crack of armaments,
A spout of blood.
Doubtless,
He went straight to heaven.

Kelly's Crag:

3 July 2018

The perennial rye grass sweeps in seamless, shimmering waves
Across that windswept, browning crag.
The soil is thin; the sun is hot.
It's 32 degrees, the water table's low.
The news informs us of the farmers' perilous lot.

The startled sheep's bouncy flight—
Heads held jauntily on high—
Cross the peeping rocks.
How keenly they take fright.

Species' depletion across the globe.
These are scientific facts.
The damage continues,
Assisted by mindless kleptocrats

Not prepared to act
To stall the rising tide.

Settled Bread and Craven A

Childhood treats
On vacant streets.
The harried bee has long since gone.
The fairy thimble's
Vanished.
Another time,
Another day,
When potatoes grew in troubled fields.

I need some settled bread.
The turkey stuffing must be made.
She needs a smoke,
And Craven A is best;
They're softer on the throat.
They're filtered;
They're better than the rest—
Or so the advertisers say.

I heard a voice come through the hazel wands,
'How many did you get today?'
'None,' sez I, and I looked the other way.
'I don't believe you.
Show me your hand.
Ah, there they are,
The tell-tale marks
Of the teacher's brutal wand.'

'You didn't learn your Irish then.
Your tables got all mixed up.
The teacher reeks of drink,
And Clara won the cup.'

He drove the very reverend's Vauxhall car;
The latter always in the back.
Like the queen, he rode.
He waves,
He smiles,
Royalty by another code.

The Triumph of Nothingness

Eclectic tastes
And Dire Straits
Shaped a jammed-up life's ambition.
Here and there,
As pressure grew,
He feared the worst
And then delivered
A wayward act of contrition.

It's those metaphysical things,
Those metaphysical strings and slings,
That ensure we're kept to heel.
And then there's conflict
Of a useless kind.
Devoid of meaning,
Devoid of purpose,
Nodding on
A Pavlovian sea.

It was Sunday again,
When excited children dunked hardened biscuits
In Grandma's sweetened tea.

Churros in a Chiringuito

The grey Med churned fine-grain sand
In the strong wind.
The mistral wind,
The foam … *whoosh*, it tells a story.
The soapy, sudsy bubbles split the light—
Red, orange, green, blue, indigo,
Violet.

White light split.

The edges flap.
The punters talk.
The incessant sounds of cackle
Are no match for nature.
Flap, flap, *whoosh*, grey
Skies portend a summer downpour.
Indispensable vapour,
Soil enriching,
Soil dampening,
Soil invigorating,
Life-giving, *whoooosh*.

Discarded aluminium cans
Flattened on a troubled beach.
Polyethylene everywhere.
Man is the measure of all things:
Ah yes, man is the measure of all things!

'There's good fishin'
There they say.'
'Where?'
'In the porcupine bank.'
'And where is that now?'
'Away from here.
In the Atlantic Ocean.'

'No, dada, there!'

'Oh my God.
There's great fishin' here,
I dab daily and pull a dada.'
'What's that?'
'Is that a dorada?' I ask.
'Great in salt.
It's factoried now.'
'Wha?'
'The fishin.'

'Oh, right!'

And he wandered on his way
Past the parasols,
Past the sun-baked tourist,
Head not right.
He soon vanished out of sight.

Anzac Memory, April 1915

He shall not hear the tui songs again.
He'll not plough in Northland's fertile soil,
Nor mow the hay
Nor live another day.

The Turkish guns
Will see to that.
Falling comrades,
Blood spilled in vain,
Filled the hours in Anzac Cove.

The screams of pain,
The dying moans
Of comrades from
The Bay of Plenty,
Waipa,
And so many loving homes.

Where is he now?
No news came, no letters land
In Matarangi or Taranaki
Informing of the nightmarish evil hand.

Phosphorus Bombs on the Gaza Strip

Tearful, fearful eyes,
Hair in dusty, curly knots,
Legs crossed in fearful stance,
Snuggled into mum.
Daily trots,
Elemental, virus-enriched snots.

Fundamental dust,
Encrusted blood.
Twisted steel,
Concrete slabs,
Broken and cracked by misplaced zeal

Of a tyrannical state,
Killing hungry, malnourished children,
Deciding their fate
With American bombs
Fuelled by racial hate.

So cretinously absurd,
The holocaust victims'
Memories blurred
By ignorance, conceit,
And narcissism.

And orphans die.

Hamilton Gardens, 18 February 2019

The peaceful noise of cheeping cycads
Filling the drowsy, humid air—
Gene driven.
A mallard floats on by, searching.
A fantail flits from branch to branch,
Too fast for me to catch
An image.
Meanwhile,
A tui sings his diverse songs.

The camellias are dull now; it's
Too late to catch their winter beauty,
Nurtured by the human waste
Casually placed in Irishtown,
Wastefulness uncontrolled.

Uncaring civilized man again
Insults the native gods,
Commoditizing the very breath of life.

Holding Back the Tide

Hair thinning,
Crows' feet deepening,
Joints aching,
Protruding puku,
Restless, gappy nights.

Memory games
Distort the past.
The Gemini guesses,
Impulsive,
Hairs plucked,
Creases filled with
Toxic, wrinkle fillers.

The forecast was not good.
I must bring in the washing.
The Kiwis got a thrashing
On a crease.

That can't be filled
With *Clostridium botulinum*.

The Living Wind

An Séadán Sí

Had a word with the wind today,
But she ignored my call.

I often call her names
When she dares to blow my hair

Or disturb the plastic
On the rick, held down tight.

I often listen in the night
To her whiney, chimney noises.

Her whistles,
Her slate-lifting goings-on.

She's a mistral,
She's a westerly,
A polar easterly,
Tropical too,
And passing.
And sometimes lasts too long.

She takes many forms
And lashes trees and streets,
And meets the rain at my front door.

She's a trade.
She's prevailing now,
Coming from the side
With the rising tide.

Alone and Old

When you're alone and old
And find a stain upon a chair,
And days have passed,
You've no one to ask
About the mark
Or where you've been
Or if it's been seen
Upon your seat
In broad daylight,
In the busy street.

Do I turn left or right?
Oh, where in Christ's name am I now?
Should I be home or away?
Did I forget to shave today?

Which way did I come?
Where's she gone?
She's not around;
Our paths have crossed
So many times before.

Oh, my God, I'm lost.

A Snifter Break

A pint and a ball of malt
In Connolly's of Dunbell.
I need something to warm the gut.
It's been a hard day,
And I'm not feeling very well.
The toil is rough.
It's like the
Never ending fuchsia fields tethered to the ocean.
Scythe swish after swish,
Tractor-challenged land.
Soft,
Fern riven, sour; why?

The pee haich is low
Caused by anaerobic fermentation.
And a bovine station,
Close-by yesterday,
Drowning the nation in methane
From eating grass and hay.

As he downs another ball of malt to ease the pain.

A Childhood Dream:

Part of a Conversation Overheard, Dublin 1970

If I could pick me ma,
I'd pick the queen.
Everywhere I'd go, there'd be a crowd.
Ooooo, ahhh, and I'd be seen
In expensive clothes
Beside a crawler
With a haughty, pointy nose
As he'd pluck sticky chewing gum from the marrow of my soul.

Me Da would say the gutter press
(The *Sun*, the *Star*, and the *Express*)
Would have a ball,
And I'd have ice cream every day, an' all.

Free trips to here and there
On some urgent business of the time.
And important people from God knows where,
Genuflecting, bowing like a syncopated hime.
Not to mention the massive dole;
'Paid to those in castles', Dad says,
'Taxpayers' money going down a hole.
They don't give a damn 'bout society's ills,
Citizens without recourse,
Living hard on pills.'

But may I digress?

There's no going back to that sacred place.
There's no going back to the bower of song.
That's no way to say goodbye, for God's sake.
I must have meant more to you than that.
I should have got the sack
For deviating from our gilded track.

You've gone to ashes, man.
What about that secret chord?
The minor fall,
And the major lift
Ah, why should I bother now?

It doesn't matter.
It's over.
I carry the can because I outlived you.
'That's no excuse', you say.
'It's a cop-out.'
Don't be such a darned hypocrite.
I have everything I need.
I'm crazy for love.

I've missed out.

End of digression.

The palace is empty.
They're making a match.
My wish is for a strange tavern
With music by Christy,
By Leonard, or by Satch.

I've tattooed my crotch;

It won't be seen.
I have upped it by a notch.
I depart from the heritage
Of a licentious life,
A heritage of mistresses,
Of incestuous relationships,
And *prima noches*.
You're a hypocrite.
You're not one of us.
I feel guilty again.
I'm now insane
With incestuous blood.

Where's the Chelsea Hotel,
Where I can become
Anonymous while I sponsor the mammals on the parched savannah?

I didn't think that this was any way to say goodbye.

Where's my slice of civilisation?
It's in the V and A,
In the priceless treasures of the palace,
The Hogarth's, and the rest
That adorn the walls and empty spaces
In her royal highness's well-feathered nest.

Winter Fuel

It saw us through a winter.
Nay, two.

The Sylvester Pine,
Where the magpie built
Her scrappy nest
With silver paper
And the rest.

Neighbourhood 'scaldies' disappear
Through a pica, pica pest,
Stolen.

While needles grope
For space upon the ground
To acidify the soil
And overturn
Honest labour's toil.

The pale mauve flames
Dart up the blackened glass,
Leaving a trail of acrid smoke
Behind and warming
The innards of the room.
And pass, he says,
When I change the channel
And destroy his hope
Of yet another violent, noisy soap.

A Foolish Enterprise

Today I felt inadequate,
Just like yesterday,
And felt so alone,
As if I could never atone
For the sins of youth
And the rotten fruit
So thoughtlessly left behind.

Swan Lake Conversations:
Rotorua, February 2020

Had I heard of Coole?
Legend has it, I came from there,
Changed colour somewhere along the way,
Emigrating to a far-flung, foreign bay.

'I became a migrant, you know,
From distant, ancient shores.
It's not a myth, I say,
Just because I'm black from over there
Is no reason to deprive me of my rights
And stab me in the back,
Like a Windrush nightmare.'

I come from royal stock—
The Children of Lir,
Who left Loch Dairebhreach
After three hundred years
Of pain.'

A committee was set up.
What should we do with this enigmatic bird,
So carelessly blown off course?
The office ponderously
Discussed the case.
We're running out of time
In this race against
A trying foreign force.

'Let's send him home,'
The minister said.
But where is home?
Is it Toxteth, Chelsea, or Marylebone?

Does it matter now?
I'm in a gracious place
Where no one gives a damn
About the colour of my face
Or where I'm from
Or if I've fallen from ancestral grace.

When I Was Ten

Tommy, I remember it clearly,
You being beaten savagely about the head
For saying 'grub' instead of 'bread'—
The sands of time have not diminished my pain—
For when you fed the crows before going to a restful bed
Some long summers' evenings ago.

'Sentences couldn't start with "and"'.
The master said.
'You clown, you fool,
With nothing in your head.
Go home and pick the spuds
For you're good for nothing else.
You should be dead'.

Did the master have to be so cruel?

And so it was sixty years ago,
In classrooms full of intellectual challenges,
With hurling in the yard
And in winter, full of snow,
And severe shortages of oranges.

Looking at a Mansion

Bricks and mortar
Laid by tough, knurled hands.
Stairs carved by skilled, demanding men.
Holes drilled with precision
And vision when he sang

'Hey Mr. Tambourine Man'
In Newport in '64.
It's time for tea,
It's time for me,
To take a break.
But he ran away
To sing,
Not to build a mansion
But to wake us up
From our dogmatic slumbers

While we're fixing pseudo-problems
Set by wasteful genuflectors.

Filtering Out the Lies:
Autumn in Cambridge, March 2020

The giant oaks begin to shed their leaves.
The conkers mature lately in the trees.
The Spanish chestnut yields its fruit
Copiously, wastefully underfoot.

Who knows what secrets these seeds hold
Hidden in their shells?
While Mother Earth battles on,
Redressing in some small measure
The profligacy of man.

Avarice seems unbounded.
The wealthy never have enough.
They don't like the truth.
They don't like scientific work
Known as fake news stuff.

The gullible believe the narcissist
Who has never read a book.
You can see the movements in the hands;
He has that vacant look.

Mendacity is his stock in trade.
They condemn unwelcome truths,
Persecute the messenger,
Ignoring cogent roots

Of conscience.
The truth is what I say it is.
No more following of ancient rules,
No less
Consequent on the whims of fools.

About the Author

Martin Knox Publishing Bio and Background

The Knox family weren't materially well off, but love abounded. Martin Knox was born on the 22nd of April 1946, in Kilkenny, Ireland. He went to school to Clara primary school, also in Kilkenny, when he was 5 years old, walking five miles per day through farms and fields to learn the basics of reading writing and arithmetic. There was a lot of emphasis on Irish and religion in primary school in those days and this hasn't changed that much. The environment in school was brutal and threatening; really scary at times. All primary schools in Ireland in those days were controlled by the major religions, Catholicism (the Vatican), Protestantism (a less centralized agglomeration of various groups doctrinally different from each other). To this day, in the main, primary schools continue to be controlled by the bishops: there are some exceptions however. Yet nobody speaks out about this anomaly, or at least very few do, including the government. Indoctrination and good mental health are incompatible.

On the first Sunday of September 1959 Martin Knox went to Castletown Co. Laois, Ireland to begin training for a life of prayer and teaching with the De La Salle brothers. These years of 'formation' as they were subtly called were to last until he left the organization ten years later having completed the Intermediate Certificate and the Leaving Certificate (state secondary school examinations) in between. In 1967 Martin went to University College Dublin (UCD) to pursue a degree in science, majoring in Chemistry. The minor subject pursued was mathematics.

In 1990 he graduated with a PhD in physical chemistry under Professor David Feakins who had a deep love of chemistry and Beethoven. The freedom and excitement associated with the pursuit of original research cannot easily be put into words.

Looking back on the education path taken and on reflecting on childhood and adult experiences, it is hard to escape the conclusion that 'education' is designed to make the recipient into a product of some kind subservient to established order, whether in language, history, ideas, politics, religion, and mathematics even. Independence of thought and expression was not the primary focus of the endeavour. On the contrary there was no room for agnosticism and of course, atheism was totally beyond the pale: atheists were all destined for hell. Dogma was core to education, take it or leave it: a type of Hobson's choice, indoctrination or damnation. Honesty, particularly intellectual honesty was eschewed. Honesty wasn't valued: we weren't educated to be honest, either with ourselves or others.

Following graduation Martin Knox, as a De La Salle brother, taught secondary school science and mathematics, again in Dublin while doing research for a PhD degree. The experience was most exciting. It was easy to keep one's head below the parapet when teaching science and mathematics. Regrettably, I never questioned authority in any real way because the prospect of losing one's livelihood was real.

In the mid-seventies Martin Knox was engaged to lecture in chemistry in the Institute of Technology, Athlone, Ireland. Those twelve years proved to be very challenging indeed.

I late 1980's he joined big pharma in Co Clare Ireland and remained there for fifteen years – a most enjoyable experience where creativity was encouraged and rewarded mostly, though one's intellectual property was owned and profited from by big pharma.

Subsequently Martin Knox became self employed as a consultant in water management, quality, safety and environmental auditing.

He began writing poetry while visiting northern Spain in 2012 with his partner of many decades, Ann O'Connell from Killimer, Co. Clare.

My colleague and fellow poet, Conor Farrell considers my writing to be too serious and that I need to include more romantic poetry in my endeavours. However, I'm inclined to go by what Simon Armitage holds: the writer must, in his/her writing underline and reflect the social context of the times we live in. I don't always hold with that counsel: there is a place also for other stories away from the darkness.

Martin has four children and five even more beautiful grandchildren.

Lightning Source UK Ltd.
Milton Keynes UK
UKHW010625110820
368051UK00001B/227